HEINEMANN CHILDREN'S REFERENCE
a division of Heinemann Educational Books Ltd
Halley Court, Jordan Hill, Oxford OX2 8EJ

OXFORD LONDON EDINBURGH
MELBOURNE SYDNEY AUCKLAND
MADRID ATHENS BOLOGNA
SINGAPORE IBADAN NAIROBI HARARE
GABORONE KINGSTON PORTSMOUTH NH(USA)

ISBN 0 431 00312 2

British Library Cataloguing in Publication Data
Bailey, Donna
    Fishing.
    1. Angling
    I. Title   II. Series
    799.1'2

Editorial consultant: Donna Bailey
Designed by Richard Garratt Design
Picture research by Jennifer Garratt

Photographs:
Cover: Tony Stone Worldwide (Ambrose Greenway)
Peter Greenland: title page, 2, 3, 4, 5, 6, 7, 8, 9, 10, 11, 12, 13,
    14, 15, 16, 17, 18, 19, 20, 21, 22
Sporting Pictures: 23
Stephanie Colasanti: 32
Tony Stone Worldwide: 24 (Robert A Mitchell), 25, 26 (Robin
    Smith), 31 (Zeynep Sumen), 27, 28, 29, 30

Printed in Hong Kong

90 91 92 93 94 95 10 9 8 7 6 5 4 3 2 1

Fishing

Donna Bailey

HEINEMANN

Dad gave me a fishing rod for my birthday.
We're going fishing today.

We find a good spot on the river bank.
Dad takes out a box of maggots.
We will use them for bait.

I get my rod ready first.
Dad shows me how to fix the reel
to the rod.

Then I thread the nylon line from
the reel through the little holes
on the rod and out at the top.

Dad puts a maggot on the hook
at the end of the line.

I try a cast, but I forget
to take the catch off the reel so
the line does not go very far.

I reel the line back in again.
Fishing is not as easy as it looks!

Perhaps if I go up a bit higher
I can cast my line further out.
I get in a muddle so Dad helps me.

This time I get it right.
My float is right out in the river.

I sit down to watch the float.
Dad says if it bobs up and down
a fish is on the end of the line.

I think the float is bobbing.
I reel the line in quickly but
there's nothing there.

I cast the line out again.
I'm getting better at it now.

I can feel a tug on the line and
my float is bobbing up and down.
Dad helps me reel in my line.

Look! I've caught a fish!
It's the first one I've caught
with my new rod.

Dad grabs the net and scoops up
the fish onto the bank.

Dad takes the hook out of its mouth.
The fish is so small that we throw it
back into the river.
Dad puts another maggot on my hook.
Fishing is good fun!

This man has just caught a nice big trout
in the river.

He doesn't use maggots for bait but flies made from feathers.

He chooses a fly and ties it to
the end of his line.

His fishing rod is very light and bendy.
It helps him cast the fly and trail it
lightly over the top of the water.

He wades out into the river and casts
the fly where he thinks a fish is hiding.
This is called fly fishing.

These people are in a fishing competition.
The person who catches the biggest fish wins.

This man is fishing from the beach at the seaside.
His rod is big and strong to pull the fish through the waves.

This fisherman has just caught
a blue marlin from his boat.

He is strapped into a special chair so the big fish cannot pull him overboard.

The fishermen on this boat go out
every day to catch fish.
They do not go fishing for fun.
It's their job.

The fishermen lower nets to catch the fish.
They lay the nets across the sea bed or
pull the nets along behind the boat.

Even in winter these fishing boats
leave port to go and catch herring.

The fish are pulled aboard and put
in the ship's hold until the boats
go back to port.

These fishermen are selling their fish
on the dockside.

Other fishermen send their fish
to markets or supermarkets.

Index